If you were a

Homonym
or a Homophone

by Nancy Loewen
illustrated by Sara Gray

PICTURE WINDOW BOOKS
Minneapolis, Minnesota

homonym two words that are pronounced and spelled the same but have different meanings

homophone two words that are pronounced the same but have different spellings and different meanings

Special thanks to our advisers for their expertise:

Rosemary G. Palmer, Ph.D., Department of Literacy
College of Education, Boise State University

Susan Kesselring, M.A., Literacy Educator
Rosemount–Apple Valley–Eagan (Minnesota) School District

Editors: Christianne Jones and Dodie Marie Miller
Designer: Tracy Davies
Page Production: Lori Bye
Art Director: Nathan Gassman
The illustrations in this book were created with acrylics.

Picture Window Books
5115 Excelsior Boulevard
Suite 232
Minneapolis, MN 55416
877-845-8392
www.picturewindowbooks.com

Printed in the United States of America.

Library of Congress Cataloging-in-Publication Data
Loewen, Nancy, 1964–
If you were a homonym or a homophone / by Nancy Loewen ; illustrated by Sara Gray.
p. cm. — (Word fun)
Includes bibliographical references and index.
ISBN-13: 978-1-4048-3161-2 (library binding)
ISBN-10: 1-4048-3161-4 (library binding)
ISBN-13: 978-1-4048-3571-9 (paperback)
ISBN-10: 1-4048-3571-7 (paperback)
1. English language—Homonyms—Juvenile literature. I. Gray, Sara, ill. II. Title.
PE1595.L64 2006
428.1—dc22   2006027306

Looking for homonyms and homophones?

Watch for the **big, colorful words in the example sentences.**

Editor's Note: Homonyms and homophones are closely related, but they are not the same thing. Homonyms are discussed in the first part of the book, and homophones are discussed in the second part of the book.

If you were a homonym ...

3

... you could **BARK** at the **BARK,** while you **COAST** along the **COAST.**

4

You could **ROLL** with your **ROLL** and

TOAST with your **TOAST**.

5

If you were a homonym, you would be spelled and pronounced the same as another word, but you would have a different meaning.

MAY I go on vacation in **MAY**?

He **CAN** drink from that
CAN faster than anyone!

World Records

If you were a homonym, you would need clues
like pictures or words to make sense.

This **LIGHT** is
not very **LIGHT**.

The **LEAN** pig could **LEAN** on a friend.

If you were a homophone ...

... you'd grow **HOARSE** yelling at your **HORSE**.
"**HEY!** Don't eat all of that **HAY!**"

If you were a homophone, you would be pronounced the same as another word, but you would have a different spelling and a different meaning.

He waved his **SHOE** to **SHOO** away the pesky bug.

The wind **BLEW** the **BLUE** balloons away.

Sam wants to **MARRY** the very **MERRY MARY**.

If you were a homophone, you could be a contraction. A contraction is two words that are combined into one. In a contraction, at least one of the letters is replaced by an apostrophe.

YOU'RE and YOUR are often confused. YOU'RE means you are. YOUR means that something belongs to you.

YOU'RE supposed to wear **YOUR** red shirt for the family picture.

If you were a homophone, you would need to be spelled correctly for the sentence to make sense. THERE, THEIR, and THEY'RE are commonly confused.

For example,
THERE means a place.
THEIR shows possession.
THEY'RE is a contraction
for they are.

THEY'RE riding **THEIR** bikes over **THERE.**

17

If you were a homophone, you could be a number but sound the same as another word.

He went **TO** the store **TO** buy **TWO** jugs of milk. He bought some juice, **TOO**.

She was the
only **ONE** who
WON the spelling bee.

Be ready **FOR**
the show by
FOUR o'clock.

If you were a homonym or a homophone, you could work together.

He **ATE EIGHT** jars of **JAM**

as he sat in the traffic **JAM**.

You would be the same and still be different ...

...if you were a homonym or homophone!

Fun with Homonyms and Homophones

Come up with a total of 10 homophones and homonyms. On 10 separate pieces of paper, write a word on one side and its definition on the other. For example, the definition of *two* would be "a number." Put the 10 pieces of paper in a bowl.

Take turns picking a word from the bowl and saying the word out loud. Make up a sentence using the word. Have other players write down the word and whether it is a homonym or homophone. When everyone has guessed, reveal the correct spelling.

Players get one point for every correct answer. When all of the words have been chosen, the player with the most points wins!

Tip: Here's a good way to remember which is which. The "nym" in homonym means "name." Homonyms are words with the same name. They are spelled the same. What do you do on a phone? You talk and listen. Homophones are words that sound alike.

23

Glossary

bark— loud crying of a dog; hard covering of a tree

hoarse—having a harsh-sounding voice

homonym— one of a pair (or group) of words that look and sound alike, but have different meanings

homophone— one of a pair (or group of words) that sound alike, but that are spelled differently and have different meanings

lean—having little or no fat; to bend or tilt

merry—happy

pesky—bothersome

toast—to honor someone; bread that has been heated and browned

To Learn More

At the Library

Cleary, Brian P. *How Much Can a Bare Bear Bear? What Are Homonyms and Homophones?* Minneapolis: Millbrook Press, 2005.

Maestro, Giulio. *What's Mite Might? Homophone Riddles to Boost Your Word Power!* New York: Clarion Books, 1986.

Rondeau, Amanda. *Bella Blew Blue Bubbles.* Edina, Minn.: Abdo Pub., 2002.

On the Web

FactHound offers a safe, fun way to find Web sites related to this book. All of the sites on FactHound have been researched by our staff.

1. Visit *www.facthound.com*
2. Type in this special code: 1404831614
3. Click on the FETCH IT button.

www.FactHound.com

Your trusty FactHound will fetch the best sites for you!

Index

homonyms
    examples of, 3-9, 20-21
    tip, 23
homophones
    contractions, 14
    examples of, 11-21
    numbers, 18
    tip, 23

Look for all of the books in the Word Fun series:

If You Were a Conjunction

If You Were a Homonym or a Homophone

If You Were a Noun

If You Were a Palindrome

If You Were a Preposition

If You Were a Pronoun

If You Were a Synonym

If You Were a Verb

If You Were an Adjective

If You Were an Adverb

If You Were an Antonym

If You Were an Interjection

24